JET COMBAT

Osprey Colour Series

JET COMBAT

Hot and high, fast and low

Ian Black

Published in 1988 by Osprey Publishing Limited
27a Floral Street, London WC2E 9DP
Member company of the George Philip Group

British Library Cataloguing in Publication Data

Jet combat: hot and high, fast and low.
  —(Osprey colour series).
  1. Fighter planes—Pictorial works
  2. Jet planes, Military—Pictorial works
  I. Black, Ian
  623.74´64   UG1242.F5

ISBN 0-85045-839-0

Editor Dennis Baldry
Designed by Paul Butters
Printed in Hong Kong

Front cover Sky-shark: a Dutch F-16A from No 323 Sqn formates on an F-16B from the same unit, which is carrying a dayglo Sidewinder missile on the wingtip launcher. The squadron badge on the fin of the F-16 depicts the goddess Diana on a black disc

Title pages It will be sometime yet before the sun finally sets on the Phantom air-defenders of Nos 19 and 92 Sqns at Wildenrath in West Germany (chapter one). The F-4's replacement, the multinational Eurofighter, was still little more than a series of flickering computer-generated images as this book went to press in the winter of 1988, and it looks as though the lads at the sharp end will have to wait until the dawn of the 21st century before they can strap in to the RAF's first hi-tech single-seat fighter. When that happens, the F-4 will have been in RAF service for over 30 years

Back cover Check six!

Right A self-portrait of the author at the controls of a Lightning T.5 operational trainer

To my wife Jane and our son Timothy, and with special thanks to my brother, Stuart

Regular devotees of the Osprey Colour Series—especially those with copies of Chris Allan's *Fast Jets 1* and *2* on their bookshelves—will be happy to learn that *Jet Combat* is the product of another RAF Lightning pilot with a penchant for photography.

Flight Lieutenant Ian Black has the historic distinction of being the last pilot through the Lightning OCU (operational conversion unit) at Binbrook in Lincolnshire, where he is currently serving with No 11 Sqn on the Lightning F.6. The imminent phase-out of the Lightning means that by the time this book is published in June 1988, Ian Black will be converting to the Tornado F.3 with No 229 OCU at Coningsby.

The author joined the RAF in October 1979 and between February 1981 and February 1984, he served as a navigator on Phantoms with No 19 Sqn at RAF Wildenrath in West Germany. But by the end of his tour in Germany he was determined to become a pilot. After instruction at the Flying Selection Squadron at Swinderby (Chipmunk), No 7 Flying Training School at Church Fenton (Jet Provost), and No 4 FTS at Valley (Hawk), he was awarded his wings in February 1986. This period of training was interrupted by a short tour with the Chipmunks of No 6 Air Experience Flight at Abingdon in the spring of 1984.

After successfully completing his course at No 1 Tactical Weapons Unit at Brawdy between March–August 1986, he was posted to the Lightning Training Flight at Binbrook in September 1986.

Interestingly, his father, Air Vice Marshal George Black, CB, OBE, AFC and bar (Rtd), was a Lightning pilot with Nos 74 (Tiger), 111 and 5 Sqns, and No 226 OCU. Brother Stuart is a Tornado navigator at Coningsby in Lincolnshire, and became the first RAF navigator to complete an exchange tour on the F-14 Tomcat with VF-101 'Grim Reapers' at Naval Air Station Oceana, Virginia, in 1982–85.

The photographs in *Jet Combat* were taken exclusively with Canon cameras and lenses, loaded with Kodachrome and Fuji film. All of the air-to-air photographs were taken during normal training flights from Phantom, Hawk, F-16 and Lightning aircraft. The views expressed in this book are the author's and do not necessarily reflect those of the Ministry of Defence or of the Royal Air Force.

Right A pair of Lightning F.6s of No 11 Sqn loom into close formation after an air-to-air gunnery sortie. The chalk marks on the fuselage of the nearest aircraft indicate the number and colour of the shells loaded, plus some artistic flair on the part of enthusiastic groundcrews

Contents

The sharp end: RAF Germany

Left A Phantom FGR.2 (F-4M) of No 19 Sqn toting the standard RAF Germany fit of 2 × 270 US gal (1400 lit) Sgt Fletcher underwing fuel tanks; a centreline SUU-23/A Vulcan cannon pod; twin-Sidewinder launch rails on the two inboard wing pylons; and a pair of Sparrow ballast rounds in the forward fuselage stations to keep the aircraft's CG (centre of gravity) within limits. This particular Phantom (XV411) has spent its entire career in RAFG, initially in strike and reconnaissance roles, but later (in common with the RAF's FGR.2 fleet) it transferred to air defence following the advent of the SEPECAT Jaguar

Above On the ramp: Wg Cdr Reg Hallam (pilot) and Flt Lt Ted Threapleton (navigator) prepare for a 2 v 2 fight with F-15 Eagles on the ACMI (Air Combat Manoeuvring Instrumentation) range in Sardinia, Italy. Interestingly, the front seater is wearing the old Mk 1 silver-coloured bonedome; though lighter and giving better all-round vision than modern headgear it provides less protection against birdstrikes and the violent windblast of a high speed, low level ejection

'Last chance' checks on the control surfaces, including flaps and speedbrakes (the latter are called airbrakes in the RAF), as the groundcrewman on the left signals to the pilot to confirm the correct operation of each of the surfaces in turn

Control stick fully back, burners lit, a final check that the outer wings are spread and locked; it's time to let the brakes off and send over 50,000 lb (23,000 kg) of Anglo-American heavy metal. down the runway at Wildenrath, one of RAF Germany's three 'clutch' airfields near the Dutch border

Airborne! Gear up, flaps up, and a final check that all warning captions are out

Right Once the Phantom is cleaned up aerodynamically the first task is to complete the pre-attack checks and arm the missiles as quickly as possible; at this stage it would be distinctly un-cool to be 'bounced' (caught by surprise) and not have the chance to make a fight of it

Our faithful Phantom cuts the edge of a cloud bank, looking for a suitable gap in which to let down before a low-level search for 'trade' (hostile aircraft)

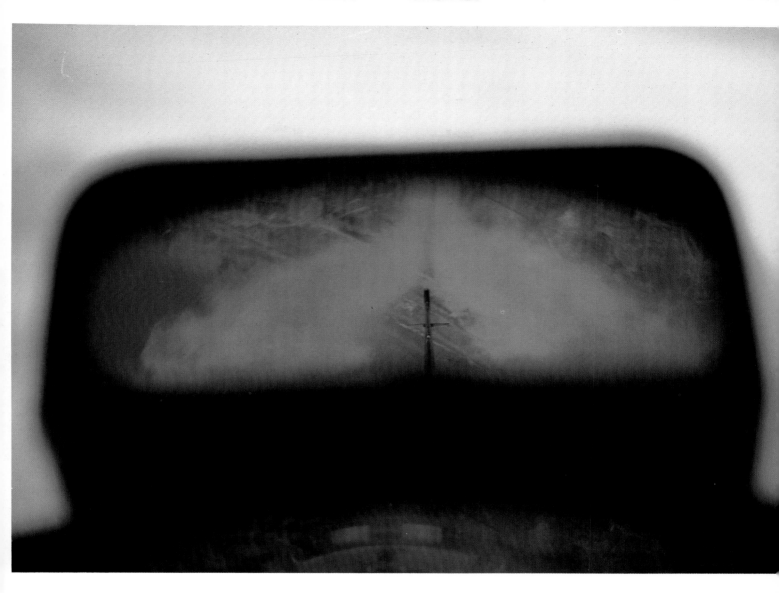

Left Sortie over, this is a navigator's eye view of the front seater checking our six o'clock one last time. Many air defence crews prefer to wear white helmets because they reduce the effects of reflected heat from the canopy at high altitudes. Unfortunately, these helmets also tend to compromise the aircraft's camouflage and in wartime a rapid tone-down would occur. Colourful squadron markings would also disappear, but in peacetime they help to maintain a sense of *esprit de corps* among aircrews

Above Pulling into a loop at 400 knots (741 km/h)—the recommended entry speed for the Phantom—as seen in the backseater's rear view mirror. The pilot and navigator each have a rear view mirror to alleviate the poor visibility from the aircraft in this direction, but if you get your first sight of the bad guy from the mirror it's often too late to react

17

Left Those tell-tale wingtip vortices indicate that this Phantom is pulling hard to get within killing range. The RAF's F-4s are limited to +7G, though 3–4G is more common in the course of normal operations to minimize fatigue damage

Above No 19 Sqn received its Phantoms in 1976, having previously operated the Lightning F.2/F.2A interceptor at Gutersloh from 1965 with No 92 Sqn, its long-standing partner which converted to Phantoms at Wildenrath in April 1977. This FGR.2 is following the coastline of the Italian Riviera en route to the annual Venice airshow in 1983

Left Classic meets classical. A Phantom dips a wing over Venice, city of commerce, fine glass, priceless art treasures and rising damp

Above Our No 2 hangs in close to the starboard wingtip as we streak across the outskirts of Venice at 250 ft (75 m). Air defenders rarely venture below this height, but Buccaneer, Jaguar and Tornado aircrew are specially cleared to train at 100 ft (30 m) as part of the work-up for exercises such as Red Flag in the Nevada desert

Top left Back to reality. There could hardly be a greater contrast to Venice than RAF Valley in North Wales. Each air defence squadron spends two weeks a year here to allow crews to fire missiles in a variety of operational conditions. This particular aircraft, serial XV481/G, is carrying a strike camera pod under the jet intake and a Bullpup missile body under the port-outer wing pylon to record the launch of a Sky Flash radar guided missile on high-speed film

Left The same aircraft in Corsica some six months later, shortly before the aircraft was repainted in air defence grey. A temporary sharkmouth has been chalked on the nose with a rendering of the famous Phantom 'Spook' on the intake. The squadron's blue and white checks have been painted on the baggage pod inboard of the fuel tank

Above Staying in sunny climes, XV439/D taxies in after a 30 minute air-to-air gunnery sortie. The pod containing the 20 mm six-barrel M61A1 rotary cannon is clearly visible under the fuselage. This long-lived and reliable weapon has an extremely high rate of fire, spitting out a full magazine of 1200 high-velocity shells in just 12 seconds

Overleaf Getting airborne from Wildenrath's rain-soaked runway for another training sortie in the spring of 1983

Top and bottom left In the '100 missions over Vietnam' tradition, final sorties or a thousand hours on type usually end with an early bath courtesy of the fire section. Many aircrew attempt to evade the fireman's hose, but few succeed

Above I think the great Charles E Brown must have been sitting on my shoulder when I took this shot of XV480/B. It's quite usual for air defence aircraft to transit at high level to conserve fuel. An attack on a low level target from this height would also be a good tactical option

27

Battle Flight, RAF Germany's equivalent to the UK's Quick Reaction Alert force. A pair of fully-armed Phantoms are maintained at immediate readiness, 24 hours a day, 365 days a year, come rain or shine. If scrambled, this aircraft and its partner would be airborne in under five minutes to intercept the intruder(s). Policing the border with East Germany involves escorting wandering airliners out of harm's way or shepherding inquisitive Warsaw Pact combat aircraft

Multi-coloured Phantom: No 92 Sqn painted two of their F-4s with light blue horizontal stabilators to aid visual recognition at low level during simulated combat. In a multiple engagement, especially when identical aircraft are involved, it is vitally important to recognize your wingman at all times—shooting him down by mistake is, to put it mildly, rather embarrassing. Pictured on 25 January 1983, XV498/R is sporting 92 Sqn's red and yellow checks and cobra badge on the fin (vertical stabilizer)

A loose Diamond Nine formation over RAF Akrotiri, Cyprus, in May 1983, led by three aircraft in air defence grey camouflage. The solitary shadow is from the tenth Phantom acting as photo chase

Overleaf Nine in a row: the luckless No 9 is only just hanging on, selecting full afterburner and idle power in quick succession to stay in formation. Phew!

Top left Gear up as 'Foxtrot' of No 19 Sqn prepares to swing out to sea to do battle with some F-5E Tiger IIs from the US Air Force's renowned 527th Aggressor Squadron. The Aggressors know every trick in the Soviet air combat manual (and some that aren't) so unless you see him first you'll almost certainly appear as a guest star in his gunsight video

Left Air-to-air gunnery sorties are flown with the drop tanks removed to reduce wing fatigue and provide a more stable gun platform. The backseater has an important role to play during air-to-air firing, calling off the range at intervals and making the vital 'break out' call if the pilot becomes over-enthusiastic and gets too close to the banner target and its Canberra tug

Above Joining into close formation for recovery. A descent through 30,000 ft (9150 m) of cloud and then getting your first glimpse of the ground at 200 ft (60 m), 1 nm (1.6 km) out from the runway threshold, is not uncommon. One tries to remain calm and perform a controlled crash right on the numbers

Winter warm-up: an FGR.2 from No 19 Sqn patrols over a carpet of snow. Fresh from the paint shop, with low-visibility roundels and less conspicuous blue and white checks, it will only retain its clean appearance for about three weeks until an accumulation of oil, jet fuel and hydraulic fluid begins to stain the aircraft

All of the RAF's Phantom FGR.2s were originally
camouflaged Dark Green/Dark Sea Grey on the
upper surfaces and Light Aircraft Grey on the
undersides in keeping with their low level strike
role. The switch to air defence in 1974 initially
brought no change in the tactical camouflage
scheme, but in 1979 the RAF officially adopted a
carefully researched grey colour scheme for air
defence aircraft and the Phantom force became
the first to use it

The same Phantom two-ship make a snappy
recovery to Decimomannu in Sardinia, the home
of NATO's only ACMI facility. Most of the action
takes place to the west of the Cap Frasca range.
The blue SN231 telemetry pod visible on the
nearest Phantom provides an accurate
simulation of Sidewinder AIM-9L launch

parameters and sends back data to powerful
computers, which then produce diagramatic
representations of the engagement on large TV
screens monitored by operators on the ground.
The course and outcome of each combat is
recorded for the subsequent 'who got who'
debrief when the crews land

As I mentioned earlier, RAF Phantoms don't
seem to stay clean for long

'Mystery Phantom?' It is actually XV422/O of No 92 Sqn being towed along the peri track at Wildenrath. In the 1960s, Phantoms were famous for gaining a string of world speed and altitude records, but this F-4's claim to fame is rather more dubious; it accidentally *shot down* a Jaguar GR.1 strike aircraft with a well-aimed Sidewinder during a training exercise in 1983. To the immense relief of all concerned, the Jaguar pilot escaped unharmed. Unlike the many victorious American and Israeli F-4s in the past, this unfortunate Phantom did not have a kill marking stencilled on the intake (or did it?!)

When this photo was taken in January 1984, the vast majority of the RAF's Phantom fleet had been retrofitted with fintip radar warning receivers (RWR), but not this grey machine from No 19 Sqn being flown by Group Captain John Allison. Today, all the Phantom FGR.2s and FG.1s in squadron service have the fintip RWR fit. The ex-US Navy F-4Js serving with No 74 (Tiger) Sqn at RAF Wattisham in Suffolk were delivered with American RWR equipment housed in distinctive fairings on the jet intakes

Right Squadron Exchange: north of the Artic Circle during a mission from Bodo in Norway, an echelon of three F-16A Fighting Falcons of No 331 Sqn, Royal Norwegian Air Force, follow a lone Phantom from No 19 Sqn through the fjords. Unlike the 'Electric Jets' supplied to the US Air Force and other export customers, Norwegian F-16s have a brake parachute built-in to the fairing above the jet exhaust nozzle to assist operations from ice covered runways

A Phantom swoops down for a closer look at a blue ice glacier in northern Norway. An ejection over this desolate and treacherous landscape would probably be a most enlightening experience—assuming one survived long enough to be rescued

Burners in on both Spey turbofans and dumping fuel from its wing vents, Phantom XV476/L punches through a gap in the darkening clouds. The navigator will be using the Westinghouse AWG-12 radar to scan high and low to check that the clouds aren't hiding anyone else. Note the dolphin badge of No 19 Sqn in the middle of the fin

Right Phantom pharewell: homeward bound, mission accomplished

Tanking

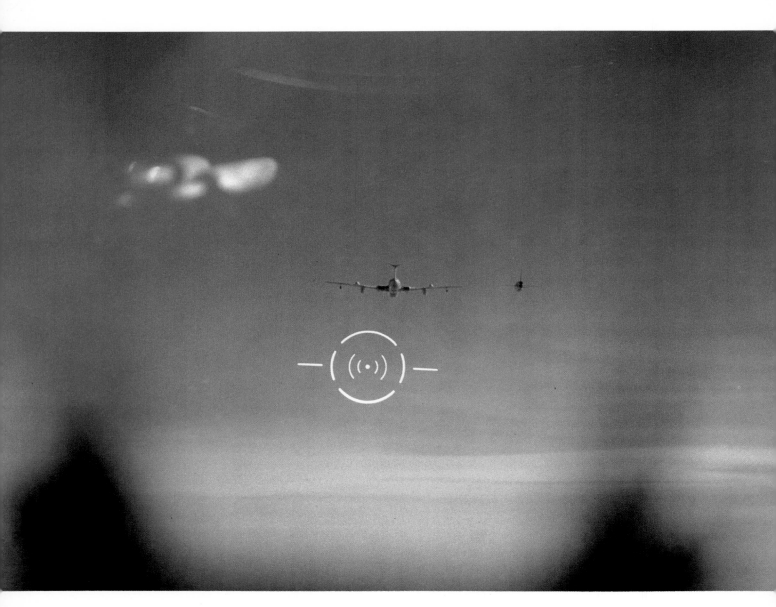

Left An enemy fighter's dream—and a tanker crew's nightmare. The 'chick' on the right would be taken first to eliminate any threat to the attacker. With no fighter cover, the tanker would then become the proverbial sitting duck

Above Surely one of the most elegant airliners ever built, the Vickers VC10 prototype made its maiden flight on 29 June 1962. Twenty-six years later this VC10 K.2 tanker trails its two wing hoses as it prepares to receive some thirsty customers. A third Hose Drum Unit (HDU) is housed under the rear fuselage. Following their retirement by British Airways and East African Airways, the RAF modified a mix of Standard and Super VC10 models (designated K.2 and K.3 respectively) to equip No 101 Sqn, which formed at Brize Norton in Oxfordshire on 1 May 1984

Top left Aerial jousting: manoeuvring a Lightning T.5 into the 'waiting position' at 300 knots (556 km/h)

Left This VC10, serial ZA147, is one of the RAF's four K.3s and was originally 5H-MMT, one of five Model 1153s purchased by East African Airways

Above This is the welcome sight that has saved many a pilot's neck in peace and war—a big, beautiful tanker with fuel to spare reeling out the basket for the receiver's hungry probe. Most fighters consume around 1000 pounds (575 lit) of fuel per minute in afterburner at low level and the chance of a quick refill is never missed. The small lights around the rim of the basket enable night refuelling, while the 'traffic lights' in the wing pods and centreline station indicate if fuel is flowing to the receiver and when his tanks are full

Top left A wide angle shot taken from the left-hand seat of a Lightning T.5 as we guzzle fuel from the tanker. Having successfully lanced the basket, in-flight refuelling is fairly straightforward if you remember to stay relaxed and keep the aircraft steady. A piece of cake—well, almost . . .

Left That's Crete down there, which means a nice long runway in the unlikely event of a refuelling mishap. Today, however, the JP4 is flowing freely and everything is in the green—Cyprus, here we come! If a problem does occur with the tanker, the receiver should have conserved enough fuel to divert to the nearest suitable airfield. Your hair can turn grey very quickly if you arrive at the tanker with below diversion fuel and something goes wrong . . .

Above The pilot's mask and helmet visor conceals the concentration required to hold station with the tanker

A pair of Lightning F.6s of No 11 Sqn flown by Sqn Ldr Paul Cooper and Flt Lt Bob Bees refuel en route to RAF Akrotiri, Cyprus, in June 1987. Bob Bees is also featured on page 46 of *Fast Jets 2*, another Osprey Colour Series volume, published in August 1987, and he is currently on exchange with the 325th Tactical Training Wing at Tyndall, Florida, flying F-15 Eagles

Right A sneaky 'down under' view of the same refuelling contact. The VC10 K.2 is powered by four Rolls-Royce Conway turbofans, each developing 20,370 lb (9240 kg) of thrust. Interestingly, the tailplane spans 33 ft 8 in (10.27 m), exactly the same as the wing span of the Hawker Hunter jet fighter

Paul Cooper and Bob Bees tag along with the VC10 as they guide their Lightnings towards Cyprus for an Armament Practice Camp (APC)

The VC10 was selected as a partial replacement for the venerable Victor, an example of which is seen here with two Phantoms taking up position behind the wing hoses. Tanking usually takes place over the North Sea unless an overseas deployment is required, but there are also special corridors over central Germany

Hawk miscellany

Left A British Aerospace Hawk T.1 from No 4 Flying Training School at RAF Valley in North Wales displays its attractive, high-visibility plumage during a tailchase over dramatic Welsh terrain. Exercises like this help the student to master the basics of 1 v 1 combat

Above If a poll were conducted to find out which aircraft was considered to be the best looker in the RAF I'm pretty sure the Hawk would win by a clear majority. Deliveries of the 175 Hawks ordered by the RAF began at Valley in November 1976 and ended when the refurbished Development Batch (DB) aircraft XX158 arrived at RAF Chivenor, North Devon, in March 1982

Sunlight races across Cymyran Bay as a Hawk comes in over the beach at Anglesey on finals for Valley. In the approach configuration the aircraft's speed is closely monitored as a matter of routine, although in the course of flight-test development two triangular-section 'breaker strips' were added to either wing leading edge to create buffet and thereby provide good natural stall warning

Test pilot trainer: the unmistakable colour scheme of a Hawk operated by the Empire Test Pilots' School at Boscombe Down in Wiltshire. Sharp-eyed readers will be able to spot the Airstream Direction Detector (ADD) vanes on the pitot-static head, but not the cassette voice-recorder, digital tape-recording system (used to record rates of rotation in pitch, roll and yaw, engine throttle setting, airspeed, altitude, etc), fuel flow meter and sensitive ASI and altimeter in the cockpit

Overleaf The Hawk is now synonymous with the Red Arrows, despite the formidable reputation established by the diminutive Folland Gnat T.1 which the team operated from 1965 until they gave their first Hawk display in November 1979. An invitation to fly with the RAF's premier formation aerobatic team is not one to be missed and I enjoyed the flight of a lifetime in the backseat of Flt Lt Guy Bancroft-Wilson's Hawk ('Red Nine')

'Smoke on': a cool 7G break back into the circuit at RAF Scampton in Lincolnshire, the Red Arrows' home base. After 40 minutes in the backseat of Red Nine, I felt as though I'd just flown two-or-three consecutive combat sorties. The Red Arrows' display may look relaxed from the ground, but I can vouch for the fact that it's hard work in the air. In particular, the dazzling Synchro Pair consume up to 10 per cent of the Hawk's allotted fatigue life in the course of a display season

Left The gear comes up as a Hawk T.1A climbs away from RAF Chivenor in Devon at the start of a low level training mission. Chivenor is the home of one of the RAF's two Tactical Weapons Units (TWUs), the other being located at RAF Brawdy in North Wales. The TWUs provide weapons training for fast-jet pilots and the syllabus includes tactical formation flying, live air-to-air and air-to-ground firing of the 30 mm Aden cannon, dive attacks with rockets and free-fall bombs, low level attacks with retarded bombs and air combat manoeuvres

Above Hawks are also used to give navigators some 30 hours' experience of fast-jet flying before they are posted to the operational conversion unit (OCU) responsible for their type conversion to front-line Buccaneer, Phantom or Tornado aircraft. This self-portrait of the author in navigator mode was taken in January 1982, during his fast-jet orientation course

Left The hill tops are masked by cloud as the Hawk near the centre of the picture threads its way down a Welsh valley during a low level attack exercise. Bad weather often forces the pilot to change his planned track, which means he must try and get to the target by an alternative route—even if it involves pulling up above the clag and letting down later on. The pressure is intense: if the pilot can't make the primary target, he has to switch to the secondary . . .

Above Gunsight on: every fast-jet pilot is a fighter pilot at heart so if he's not delivering bombs he'll have guns or missiles selected. There's no bogie in the sight today however, just a few million tons of Welsh hillside

69

Sporting its distinctive black and yellow checks, a Hawk of No 63 (shadow) Sqn from RAF Chivenor bisects a layer of colourless haze. In common with Nos 79, 151 and 234 Sqns of the TWUs, in wartime No 63 Sqn would be available to bolster the RAF's airfield defences. TWU Hawks are wired for Sidewinder and, flown by pilots like the ex-Phantom jockey at the controls of this particular Hawk, Flt Lt Dom Riley, they would give a good account of themselves in combat

Right Hawk No 203 loops as a British Airways' Concorde contrails across the Bristol Channel, New York bound

The Hawk was originally seen as a Jet Provost replacement by the RAF, although in the event it replaced the Gnat T.1 and Hunter FGA.9/T.7 in the advanced training role and weapons training role respectively. The JP's basic training slot was subsequently filled by the Shorts (neé Embraer) Tucano, which entered RAF service at Church Fenton in mid-1988. But the four Jet Provost T.4s used by No 79 Sqn at Brawdy to train forward air controllers (FACs) and familiarize foreign exchange pilots with the UK operating environment will probably survive well into the 1990s

Apart from No 79 Sqn (which also operates the Hawk T.1A), the only other RAF unit currently operating the JP.4 is No 1 School of Air Traffic Control Training at RAF Shawbury near Shrewsbury. Since this photo was taken in June 1986, No 79 Sqn's T.4s have been repainted in an air defence grey scheme. More than 200 JP.4s were built for the RAF between 1962 and 1965

A Hawk T.1A of No 234 (shadow) Sqn descends into Brawdy in typically overcast, blustery weather. Air defence grey camouflage and white Sidewinder launch rails indicate the aircraft's aggressive wartime role

Right Birdstrike! The jagged, blood-splattered hole near the wing leading-edge root of the photo chase Hawk was the result of a collision with a seagull at 450 knots (835 km/h). At high speed/low level birdstrikes are an occupational hazard; even if you manage to spot the bird it's practically impossible to take avoiding action and you simply pray that it doesn't go down the jet intake, especially if you're flying a single-engined aircraft. Taking a bird through the canopy is also bad news at the best of times, but if the pilot has neglected to lock down his helmet visor a birdstrike can have horrific consequences

Tornado: multi-role muscle

Thanks to diversions from production for the RAF, the Royal Saudi Air Force had taken delivery of 20 IDS (interdictor/strike) Tornados by the end of 1987, with another 28 to follow by 1991. As part of the huge £5 billion *Al-Yamamah* project, British Aerospace was also contracted to supply the RSAF with 24 Tornado ADVs (air defence variants), 30 Pilatus PC-9 turboprop trainers and 30 Hawk Mk 65 advanced jet trainers; the training requirement also led to the acquisition of two Jetstream 31s equipped with working replicas of the Tornado rear cockpit to train backseaters

Inset BAe Warton's deputy chief test pilot Peter Gordon-Johnson (second from left) supervises the refuelling of a Tornado IDS as the aircraft is 'turned around' before completing its ferry flight to Saudi Arabia. Before delivery, the aircraft will have had several 'shake down' flights from BAe's airfield and production complex at Warton in Lancashire to ensure that it arrives in A1 operational condition

Left Not a mis-ident, just an excuse to include a photo of an Omani Jaguar B operational trainer in similar desert warpaint. Paradoxically, despite the fact that this Jaguar is fitted with a neat, nose-mounted refuelling probe, the Sultan of Oman's Air Force is not equipped with any tanker aircraft, while the RAF, which has 44 tankers, did not fit its Jaguar two-seaters with probes even though in-flight refuelling is part of the Jaguar conversion course!

EMERGENCY RELEASE
EXPLOSIVE CANOPY
RESCUE
DANGER
ROYAL SAUDI AIR FORCE
ARMAMENT

Above and top right Accessibility to the Tornado's avionics bays is excellent, the LRUs (line-replaceable units) being placed at shoulder height for convenience. The large access panels provide welcome shade for the groundcrew, too

Right Destined for No 7 Sqn at Dharan Air Base, IDS Tornado No 764 casts a swing-wing shadow across the ramp. When translated into English, the religious inscription which appears on the green rectangle on the tail reads '*There is no God but Allah, and Muhammad is the Prophet of Allah*'. Green is the traditional colour of the Fatimid dynasty of Arabia

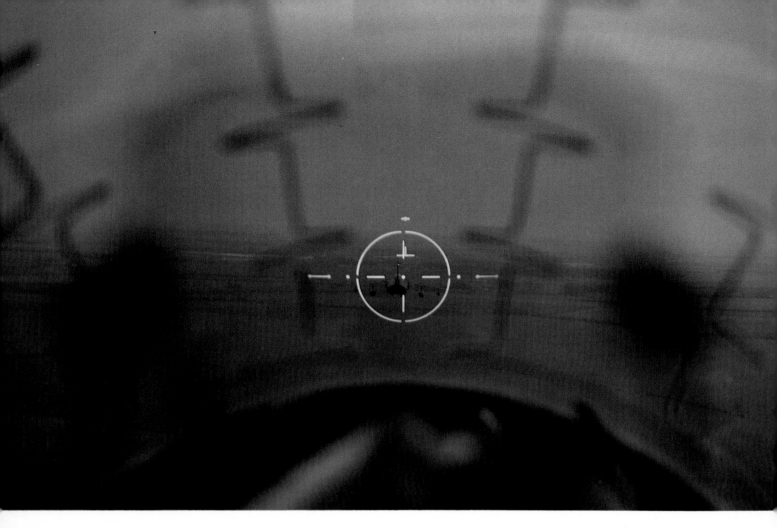

A view to a 'kill': an RAF Tornado GR.1 sits squarely in the gunsight of a Hawk after a low level bounce. This Tornado, flying straight and level in ideal guns range at roughly 450 knots (835 km/h), would be easy meat in a shooting war. However, with afterburners selected, the Tornado can outrun just about anything at low level after jettisoning its bombs

Right The distinctive markings on the fintip and foward fuselage leave no doubt that this is a Tornado GR.1 of No 617 Sqn, the unit immortalized by the May 1943 raid on the Ruhr dams in Nazi Germany. Flt Lts Keith Hargreaves (pilot) and Dave Lawson (navigator) guide their

immaculate Tornado back to base at RAF Marham in Norfolk after paying a courtesy visit to a Canadian PoW reunion at RAF Abingdon, Oxfordshire, in the summer of 1987. The store on the outboard pylon is a Marconi Sky Shadow electronic countermeasures pod, which is balanced on the opposite wing station by a Swedish-designed BOZ 107 chaff/flare dispenser. External fuel tanks are normally carried under the other two swivelling wing pylons, as here, leaving the three belly stations to carry a typical warload of 8 × 500 lb (227 kg) bombs or the massive Hunting JP233 airfield denial weapon

The German *Marineflieger* has a total of 112 Tornados, equipping two *geschwader* (MFG 1 and 2) in the anti-shipping strike role. Lacking its operational warload of up to six Kormoran anti-ship missiles, this Tornado banks over the Baltic with its wings swept fully aft at 67 degrees. **Right** The same aircraft escorted by an RAF Tornado F.3 interceptor

Hand in (wing) glove: the sleeker lines of the
Tornado F.3 compared to the shorter IDS
Tornado are apparent in these contrasting views
of the RAF/*Marineflieger* duo. **Above** A low
level pass over a Finnish-registered three-
masted Baltic Trader of 1920s vintage. **Right**
Hugging the Danish coastline

Fresh from the Warton production line, Tornado ZE162, the ninth of 147 F.3s for the RAF, cruises above picturesque French scenery in December 1986. 'AY' is on strength with No 65 (shadow) Sqn, 229 OCU, based at RAF Coningsby in Lincolnshire. With his aircraft in this configuration (i.e. clean), if the pilot chose to climb to 40,000 ft (12,190 m) and maintained full afterburner the thrust and drag curves would not meet until Mach 2.2

Right The RAF's new air-defender is fitted with a GEC Marconi AI.24 pulse-Doppler radar. In conjunction with the aircraft's well proven Sky Flash missiles, the system has reliably demonstrated long-range look down/shoot down performance against low flying targets in a heavy electronic countermeasures environment

The first operational Tornado F.3 squadron, No 29, formed at Coningsby in May 1987. This Tornado turnaround is at RAF Valley, where the antenna for the ADV's AI.24 radar is obviously in need of adjustment. In September 1987, after returning from tropical trials in Arizona, an F.3 made the first unrefuelled transatlantic crossing by a Panavia Tornado. Crewed by test pilot Peter Gordon-Johnson (see page 79) and

(see page 79)

Tornado ADV project navigator Les Hurst, the aircraft covered the 2200-nm (4075-km) distance between Goose Bay and BAe Warton in 4 hours 45 minutes. In addition to its external fuel load of two 495 Imp gal (2250 lit) and two 330 Imp gal (1500 lit) tanks, their Tornado (No AS11) was armed with four Sky Flash and the standard 27 mm Mauser cannon

Unfortunately, complex combat aircraft like the Tornado can't be given the 'kick the tyres, light the fires' treatment of yesteryear. Lengthy preflight checks are made to minimize the risk of losing vital systems (like the radar) whilst airborne

Mud-moving assortment

Left A-10 artwork: this handsome hog was painted on the *inside* of the door covering the pilot's extendible ladder to avoid compromising the European One camouflage scheme

Above A-10s from the 'Bushmasters' of the 78th Tactical Fighter Wing at RAF Woodbridge in Suffolk stand ready for a live firing mission over Cardigan Bay in West Wales. Armed with TV-guided Hughes AGM-65 Maverick air-to-surface missiles, each packing a 125-lb (57-kg) shaped charge warhead, both A-10s are also equipped with an AN/ALQ-131 electronic jamming pod (foreground) to confuse anti-aircraft defence systems

The 'Warthog' may be the slowest mud-mover in town, but it puts the *close* in close air support and is arguably one of the 'grunts' real saviours when even the tough can't get going. Teamed 'hunter/killer' style with the US Army's AH-64 Apache tank-busting chopper—which can remain concealed on the battlefield and designate targets with its advanced TV/infrared systems—the A-10 can put its bombs, bullets and Mavericks right on the money and avoid exposure to ground fire. **Left** *Silent Thunder* indeed: it's unlikely that the spin-drier whine of the A-10's TF34 turbofans will be heard above the din on the battlefield

Above Major Les Dyer formated on my Lightning to demonstrate the brisk roll rates available using the Warthog's huge split aileron/decelerons. Formerly a member of the USAF's Thunderbirds formation aerobatic team, Major Dyer serves with the 509th Tactical Fighter Squadron at RAF Bentwaters in Suffolk

Above Flt Lt Dave Sunderland waits patiently for taxi clearance in the cockpit of his Harrier GR.3 in June 1987. Tragically, he was killed only five months' later in a mid-air collision over the Otterburn bombing range, the impact also claiming the life of his No 2, an American exchange officer. Even in peacetime, the rigours of realistic training will inevitably lead to some pilots paying the highest price in the defence of freedom

Overleaf Strong sunshine reveals the complex curvatures of the Harrier's intake/nozzle area— a fine piece of tin-bashing

Above right A Harrier GR.3 of No 3 Sqn in ferry configuration with two 330 Imp gal (1500 lit) fuel tanks hung from the inboard pylons. Based at Gutersloh in West Germany, Nos 3 and 4 Sqns use the Harrier's V/STOL (vertical or short takeoff and landing) versatility in the close support role

Right The somewhat dainty appearance of the Harrier is exemplified by this Harrier T.4 operational trainer from No 233 OCU at Wittering near Peterborough, the 'Home of the Harrier' since the type entered RAF service in 1969. Armed with SNEB rocket cans and a brace of Sidewinders in addition to the standard 30 mm Aden gunpacks under the belly, the 'T-bird' can pound the ground and have a self-defence capability against fighters

These pages The new Harrier GR.5 (the RAF
equivalent to the US Marine Corps' AV-8B) is
quite different to any previous Harrier, yet it
retains the single Pegasus turbofan/four
vectoring nozzle arrangement pioneered by the
Hawker P.1127 Kestrel first flown in 1960. The
most important single improvement over the
GR.3 is the wing, which is built of advanced
composite material to save weight (some 330 lb
or 150 kg relative to an equivalent metal wing)
and features a supercritical shape to improve
lift, reduce drag and maximize fuel volume

These pages SAM-suppression is vital if the good guys plan to make a successful penetration to the target and saturate the enemy's defences. The RAF doesn't have any dedicated SAM-suppression aircraft, so in wartime it would have to rely on the USAF's Wild Weasels. This F-4G Wild Weasel serves with the 52nd TFW at Spangdahlem in West Germany and is one of 116 Weasels modified for the SAM-suppression role from low-houred F-4E models. The heart of the Weasel is its ultra-fast-reacting APR-38 radar detection and homing system, which the 'Bear' in the back seat manipulates to sniff out hostile emitters, eliminating them as required to allow the strike force to continue unmolested. The F-4G presents a dilemma to an enemy radar operator: if he continues to transmit guidance information to his surface-to-air missile batteries and anti-aircraft artillery (Triple-A), he is likely to be rudely interrupted by the arrival of Shrike or HARM (as seen above) anti-radiation missiles; if he decides to switch off, his missiles and guns will have to be fired blind. If, before switching off, the radar operator has stayed on the air long enough to be pinpointed by the Bear, he will almost certainly be taken out by a Maverick or a CBU (cluster bomb unit), or even a plain old-fashioned 500 lb (227 kg) iron bomb—the most reliable anti-SAM weapon in the business!

These pages The world's first operational variable-sweep (swing wing) aircraft, the F-111 entered USAF service in June 1967. General Dynamics' Texas swinger had to endure severe technical problems before it demonstrated its outstanding all-weather, terrain-following capabilities over North Vietnam in 1972 and emerged as the West's number one long-range interdictor. This F-111F of the 48th TFW is pictured during a sortie from its Lakenheath, Suffolk, base in October 1987. The RAF cancelled its order for 50 F-111Ks in 1966 as a result of the Government's withdrawal to west of Suez and the refocusing of its defence strategy towards Europe, where (so the argument ran) the long-range capabilities of the F-111 would not be needed

Top left The F-111E equips the 20th TFW at Upper Heyford in Oxfordshire. In common with the rest of the USAF's F-111s (some 381 airframes) the E-model is scheduled to receive its share of the $1.1 billion six-year update programme to provide new attack/terrain-following radars and new navigation, communications, IFF and electronic warfare subsystems to maintain the fleet's combat effectiveness through the 1990s. The pilot in this picture is obviously an ardent admirer of the 'Aardvark'—the nickname for the F-111

Left F-111F, tail number 74-183 of the 495th TFS/48th TFW, was one of the 18 F-111s which took part in Operation Eldorado Canyon, the American bombing raid against Libya in April 1986

Above An F-111E parked on the ramp at Upper Heyford

Binbrook: Fightertown UK

Left Tails of the unexpected? When this photo was taken on the Binbrook ramp in September 1987 the Lightning was still in the front-line of the UK's air defences, some 27 years after the first Lightning F.1s were delivered to No 74 (Tiger) Sqn at RAF Coltishall, Norfolk, in 1960. The old girl really begins to feel her age when she has to operate alongside hi-tech wonders like these Dutch F-16s, but the technology-gap didn't prevent No 11 Sqn from making a fight of it when the two classic fighters came face-to-face in a series of air combat training missions

Above No 11 Sqn's black-finned Lightning F.6 slides into close formation to emphasize the aggressive lines of the only supersonic fighter of British design and manufacture to see RAF service. When No 11 Sqn disbands on 1 May 1988 and its faithful Lightnings are variously sent to the fire dump, cut up for scrap, or dispersed to a handful of museums, the RAF will be without a single-seat fighter for the first time in its history. (*Shome mishtake shurely? Ed.*)

These pages Lightning bolt: gear travelling, burner's coming in, and no computer to limit the pilot's pull on the stick, a Lightning F.6 begins a rocket-like climb to high-level. Its partner is painted in a contrasting dark grey scheme, which is designed to camouflage the aircraft on low level intercepts over the sea

Left A Lightning F.3 of No 5(F) Sqn patrols the skies with an F.6 of No 11 Sqn. Resident at Binbrook since 1965, No 5(F) Sqn disbanded there on 1 November 1987 and travelled to Coningsby to re-equip with the Tornado F.3.

Above Flt Lt John Fynes, the last Lightning display pilot, holds station in the F.3 as Flt Lt Steve Hunt knife-edges the F.6. Both Lightnings are armed with Firestreak infrared-homing missiles

A room with a view: this is the front office of an F-16B operational trainer, occupied by 'Wimpy' of No 323 Sqn, Royal Netherlands Air Force. The only penalty incurred by the extra seat (see overleaf) is a 17 per cent reduction in internal fuel capacity

Overleaf The Brit in the back seat of this F-16B gets the benefit of a tactics recap from 'Juice', the Dutch 1000-hour F-16 pilot up front, before they blast off for a 1 v 1 fight against a Lightning. With the F-16's prolonged 9G turning ability and massive excess power, who needs tactics?

114

Left I think I'll just take this Dutch F-16 pilot's word for it! As a rule, jet fighters and women don't mix—it's either one or the other. Now, where's my F-16?

Above The cockpit of the F-16 has a Marconi head-up display (HUD), a reclining seat, a sidestick force-transducer controller linked to fly-by-wire (i.e. electric signalling) flight controls and many other advanced features. The pilot's brilliant all-round view is a major asset when it comes to 'eye-balling' an opponent in a dogfight

Overleaf 'Lightning sunset'

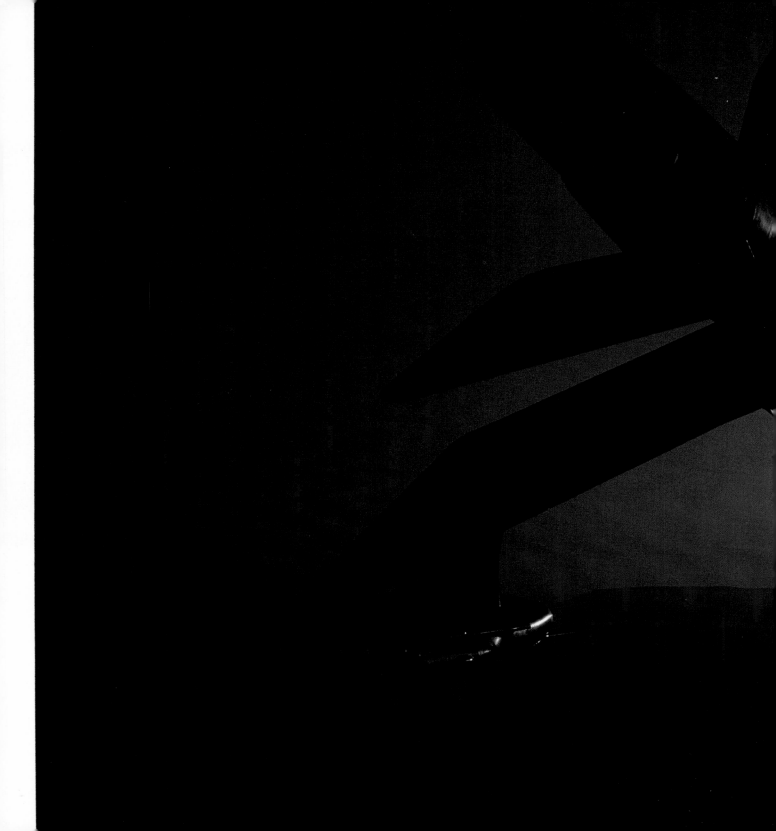

The 60-degree swept-wing and slab-sided fuselage of the Lightning reflects the state-of-the-aerodynamic-art in Britain during the early fifties, so it's hardly surprising that the Lightning looks a bit crude alongside the beautifully blended wing/body shape of GD's Fighting Falcon, which first flew on 20 January 1974—nearly 16 years after the first pre-production Lightning. What maybe slightly surprising though is the fact that the F-16 is already entering its first decade of service with the USAF. The F-16 was selected as the F-104 Starfighter replacement by Belgium, Denmark, Netherlands and Norway in June 1975

Right 'Outwards turn for combat—Go!' With two F-16s to contend with, our ace in the Lightning will have to keep the fight in the vertical plane to have any chance at all. If he breaks the golden rule and tries to turn with the F-16s he'll get smoked by a Sidewinder before he can say Fighting Falcon

Overleaf King of combat: pick a fight with the 'flying tennis court' and you'll usually have to concede game, set and match to Macair's magnificent Eagle. This F-15C, from the 32nd TFW at Soesterberg in the Netherlands, is parked at Binbrook *sans* armament and pilot during a squadron exchange in July 1987

LT. J. MORRISON
"MO"

WOLFHOUNDS

32ND

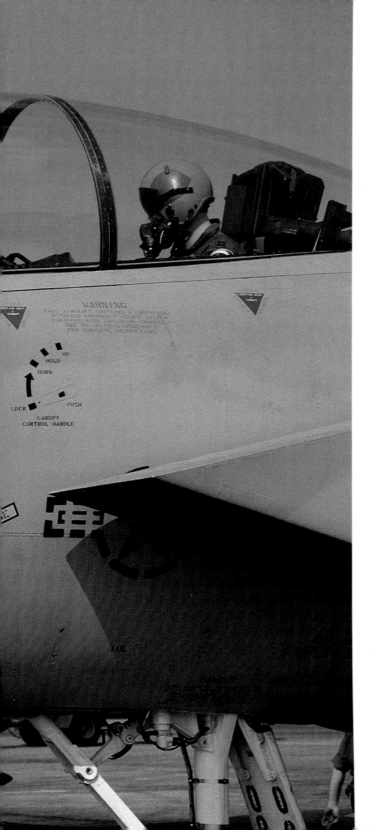

This page and overleaf Wolfmen: the pilot's of this F-15D operational trainer run-through their preflight checklists before a dissimilar air combat mission with the Binbrook Lightnings. First flown in July 1972, the Eagle is a totally uncompromised air-superiority fighter built around two extremely powerful Pratt & Whitney F100 turbofans; an incredibly sophisticated fixed-geometry wing for outstanding combat agility at subsonic speeds (which is where it really counts—you can't dogfight supersonically); and an advanced pulse-Doppler radar—initially the Hughes APG-63, but now the APG-70 on the F-15C (overleaf) and D-model with an increase in memory capacity from 24 to 96K. A typical Eagle missile mix is four radar-guided Sparrow AIM-7Fs and four infrared-guided Sidewinder AIM-9Ls. With target illumination provided by the APG-70 radar, the Sparrow missile can kill out to a range of about 20 miles (32 km), usually in a head-on pass designed to 'shoot the opponent in the face' (nasty). An M61 Vulcan cannon is carried in the bulged strake at the root of the right wing. Proof-positive of the F-15s raw power is its ability to climb vertically at supersonic speed and pull 9G manoeuvres in most parts of the flight envelope at design gross weight. Including the new F-15E Strike Eagle (392 planned), the USAF will take delivery of a grand total of 1488 F-15s, of which over 1000 are already in service